Grayslake Area Public Library District
Grayslake, Illinois

1. A fine will be charged on each book which is not returned when it is due.

2. All injuries to books beyond reasonable wear and all losses shall be made good to the satisfaction of the Librarian.

3. Each borrower is held responsible for all books drawn on his card and for all fines accruing on the same.

DEMCO

THE GREATEST PLAYERS

FOOTBALL

Megan Kopp
and Aaron Carr

MEDIA ENHANCED BOOKS
AV2
BY WEIGL™
ADDED VALUE • AUDIO VISUAL

www.av2books.com

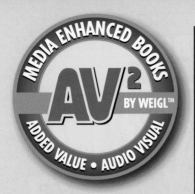

AV² provides enriched content that supplements and complements this book. Weigl's AV² books strive to create inspired learning and engage young minds in a total learning experience.

Your AV² Media Enhanced books come alive with...

 Audio
Listen to sections of the book read aloud.

 Video
Watch informative video clips.

 Embedded Weblinks
Gain additional information for research.

 Try This!
Complete activities and hands-on experiments.

 Key Words
Study vocabulary, and complete a matching word activity.

 Quizzes
Test your knowledge.

 Slide Show
View images and captions, and prepare a presentation.

... and much, much more!

Go to **www.av2books.com**, and enter this book's unique code.

BOOK CODE

J283916

AV² by Weigl brings you media enhanced books that support active learning.

Published by AV² by Weigl
350 5th Avenue, 59th Floor
New York, NY 10118
Website: www.av2books.com   www.weigl.com

Library of Congress Cataloging-in-Publication Data

Kopp, Megan.
 Football / Megan Kopp and Aaron Carr.
   p. cm. -- (The greatest)
 Includes index.
 ISBN 978-1-61690-700-6 (hardcover : alk. paper) -- ISBN 978-1-61690-705-1 (softcover : alk. paper)
 1. Football players--United States--Biography--Juvenile literature. I. Carr, Aaron. II. Title.
 GV939.A1K66 2012
 796.33092'2--dc22
 [B]
                              2011002312

Printed in the United States of America in North Mankato, Minnesota
1 2 3 4 5 6 7 8 9 0 15 14 13 12 11

062011
WEP290411

Project Coordinator Aaron Carr
Art Director Terry Paulhus

3 6109 00394 8434

Photo Credits
Every reasonable effort has been made to trace ownership and to obtain permission to reprint copyright material. The publishers would be pleased to have any errors or omissions brought to their attention so that they may be corrected in subsequent printings.

Weigl acknowledges Getty Images as its primary image supplier for this title.

Contents

Introduction

The world of professional sports has a long history of great moments. The most memorable moments often come when the sport's greatest players overcome their most challenging obstacles. For the fans, these moments come to define their favorite sport. For the players, they stand as a measuring post of success.

As one of the oldest and most popular professional sports in the United States, football has a long history that is filled with great players and great moments. These moments include Don Hutson's 83-yard **touchdown** on his first National Football League (NFL) reception and Joe Montana's third Super Bowl **Most Valuable Player (MVP)** performance. Football has no shortage of such moments, when the sport's brightest stars accomplished feats that ensured they would be forever remembered as the greatest players.

Training Camp

Football is played with 11 players on the field for each team. One team plays offense while the other plays defense. The offensive team tries to move the ball down the field to score a touchdown, while the defensive team works to prevent this.

The offense has four tries, or downs, to move the ball 10 yards. If they do this, the team is awarded a **first down**, giving them another four tries to move the ball. A touchdown is scored when a team enters the opposing team's **end zone** with the ball. Teams can also score by kicking a **field goal**.

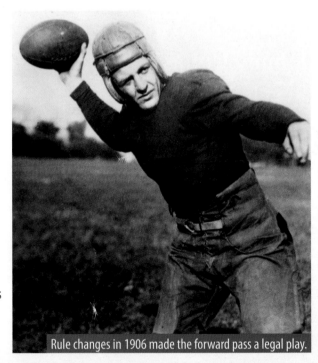

Rule changes in 1906 made the forward pass a legal play.

Football Field

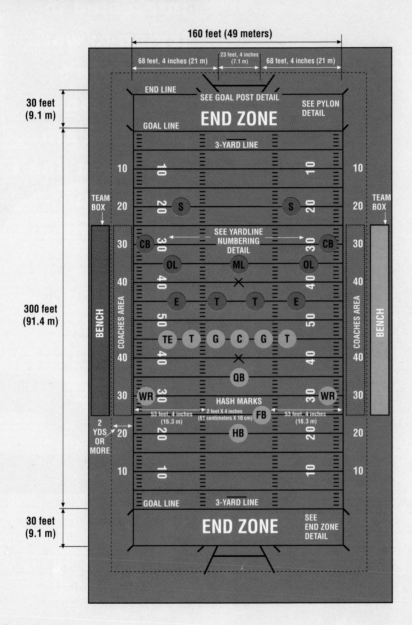

Field diagram labels

160 feet (49 meters)

68 feet, 4 inches (21 m) | 23 feet, 4 inches (7.1 m) | 68 feet, 4 inches (21 m)

30 feet (9.1 m)

END LINE
SEE GOAL POST DETAIL
GOAL LINE
END ZONE
SEE PYLON DETAIL
3-YARD LINE

TEAM BOX

300 feet (91.4 m)

BENCH

COACHES AREA

SEE YARDLINE NUMBERING DETAIL

HASH MARKS
2 feet X 4 inches (61 centimeters X 10 cm)

53 feet, 4 inches (16.3 m)

2 YDS OR MORE

TEAM BOX

BENCH

COACHES AREA

GOAL LINE
3-YARD LINE
END ZONE
SEE END ZONE DETAIL

30 feet (9.1 m)

Positions on field: S, S, CB, OL, ML, OL, CB, E, T, T, E, TE, T, G, C, G, T, QB, WR, WR, FB, HB

23 feet, 4 inches (7.1 m)
20 feet Minimum (6.1 m)
10 feet (3 m)
6 feet Minimum (1.8 m)
PADDING
GOAL POST DETAIL

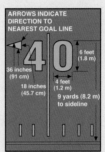

ARROWS INDICATE DIRECTION TO NEAREST GOAL LINE
40
6 feet (1.8 m)
36 inches (91 cm)
18 inches (45.7 cm)
4 feet (1.2 m)
9 yards (8.2 m) to sideline
RECOMMENDED YARD-LINE NUMBERING

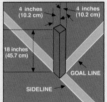

4 inches (10.2 cm)
4 inches (10.2 cm)
18 inches (45.7 cm)
GOAL LINE
SIDELINE
PYLON DETAIL

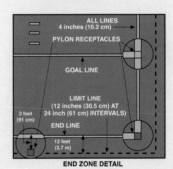

ALL LINES 4 inches (10.2 cm)
PYLON RECEPTACLES
GOAL LINE
LIMIT LINE (12 inches (30.5 cm) AT 24 inch (61 cm) INTERVALS)
END LINE
3 feet (91 cm)
12 feet (3.7 m)
END ZONE DETAIL

Player Positions

Offense

T	Tackle	G	Guard
C	Center	TE	Tight End
WR	Wide Receiver	QB	Quarterback
FB	Fullback/Runningback	HB	Halfback/Runningback

Defense

S	Safety	E	End
T	Tackle	CB	Cornerback
OL	Outside Linebacker	ML	Middle Linebacker

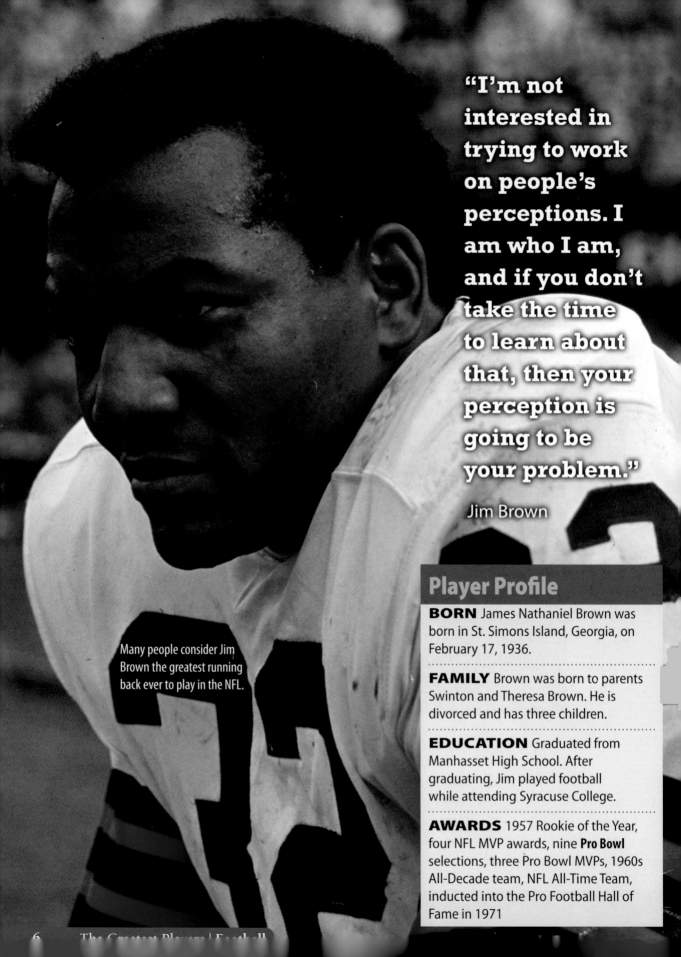

"I'm not interested in trying to work on people's perceptions. I am who I am, and if you don't take the time to learn about that, then your perception is going to be your problem."

Jim Brown

Many people consider Jim Brown the greatest running back ever to play in the NFL.

Player Profile

BORN James Nathaniel Brown was born in St. Simons Island, Georgia, on February 17, 1936.

FAMILY Brown was born to parents Swinton and Theresa Brown. He is divorced and has three children.

EDUCATION Graduated from Manhasset High School. After graduating, Jim played football while attending Syracuse College.

AWARDS 1957 Rookie of the Year, four NFL MVP awards, nine **Pro Bowl** selections, three Pro Bowl MVPs, 1960s All-Decade team, NFL All-Time Team, inducted into the Pro Football Hall of Fame in 1971

Jim Brown
Fullback

Early Years

Jim Brown's father was a professional boxer. He left the family when his son was born. Brown was raised by his great-grandmother in Georgia while his mother moved to New York to work. At eight years of age, Brown joined his mother in Long Island, New York. She was working there as a maid. He soon became involved in a gang, but he later left the gang to pursue sports.

Brown is best known as a football player. In high school, however, he also played basketball, baseball, lacrosse, and track and field. He was good enough in track and field that he considered competing in the 1956 Olympic decathlon. Brown earned All-American honors in both football and lacrosse while in college.

Developing Skills

From 1957 to 1965, Brown played for the Cleveland Browns. He led the NFL in rushing a record eight times. At 6 feet 2 inches tall and 232 pounds, he was bigger than most linebackers at the time. He was also bigger than the defensive backs who tried to **tackle** him.

Over his career of nine years and 118 games, Brown never missed a game. He ran 237 yards in one game twice. Once, he scored five touchdowns in a game, and he scored four touchdowns in a game four times.

Brown retired at the top of his game in 1966 at age 30. At that point, no other player had ever recorded as many yards (12,312) or scored more touchdowns (126) or rushing touchdowns (106).

Jim Brown

Greatest Moment

One of Brown's greatest moments came in 1965, when he became the first football player in NFL history to score 100 career rushing touchdowns. His record of scoring 100 touchdowns in just 93 games stood for more than 40 years.

Jim Brown is the only running back in NFL history to average more than 100 rushing yards per game. His average of 5.22 yards gained per attempt ranks as second highest of all-time.

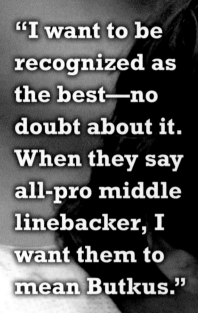

"I want to be recognized as the best—no doubt about it. When they say all-pro middle linebacker, I want them to mean Butkus."

Dick Butkus

In 1970, *Sports Illustrated* called Dick Butkus "the most feared man in the game."

Player Profile

BORN Richard Marvin Butkus was born on December 9, 1942, in Chicago, Illinois.

FAMILY Butkus was the youngest of eight children. He married his high school sweetheart, Helen, in 1963. They have one daughter, Nicole, and two sons, Richard and Matthew.

EDUCATION Butkus graduated from Chicago Vocational High School. Later, he attended the University of Illinois.

AWARDS Defensive Player of the Year in 1969 and 1970, eight Pro Bowl selections, All-Decade team for the 1960s and 1970s, NFL All-Time Team, inducted into the Pro Football Hall of Fame in 1979

Dick Butkus
Linebacker

Early Years

By fifth grade, Dick Butkus knew he wanted to be a football player. Driven to be the best, he trained hard and played fiercely. In high school, he played fullback and linebacker. It was in high school where he learned to strip the ball from runners when making a tackle. This would become one of his trademark moves.

In 1961, Butkus began playing for the University of Illinois. He quickly proved that he knew how to be at the right place at the right time. In 1963, he made 145 tackles and forced 10 **fumbles**. His play helped lead Illinois to the **Big Ten Championship**. His skills were noticed, and Butkus was drafted by the Chicago Bears.

Developing Skills

Standing 6 feet 3 inches tall and weighing 245 pounds, Butkus was a dominant defensive player. He was one of the first NFL linebackers who could defend against a run or a pass with equal effectiveness. In his rookie season, he led the Bears in fumble recoveries and **interceptions**.

Before each game, Butkus searched for something that would make him angry. He often imagined opposing players laughing at him. This helped Butkus prepare for the game. He quickly gained a reputation for intimidation and forcing fumbles, which he often recovered.

In nine NFL seasons, Butkus took the ball away from the other team 49 times. He recovered 27 fumbles and intercepted 22 passes. He was known for his physical play and pounding one-on-one contact. Knee injuries forced Butkus to retire in 1973.

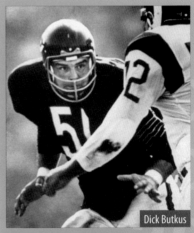

Dick Butkus

Greatest Moment

Butkus's first game with the Chicago Bears stands out as one of his greatest moments. The Bears' defense was struggling. Along came the rookie with a passion for hitting. Butkus made 11 tackles in the game.

It was not just luck, however. His skill and determination helped move the Bears up in the league standings that year. The Bears improved from a sixth place finish the year before to a third place finish in 1965.

In 119 games played, Dick Butkus recorded 1,020 tackles, scored one touchdown, and caught two passes for extra points.

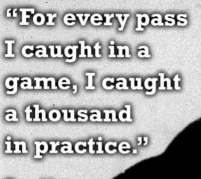

"For every pass I caught in a game, I caught a thousand in practice."

Don Hutson

Don Hutson was one of the most dominant football players of the 1930s and 1940s. Like all players during this time, Hutson played offense, defense, and even kicked field goals and extra points.

Player Profile

BORN Donald Montgomery Hutson was born on January 31, 1913, in Pine Bluff, Arkansas.

....

FAMILY Hutson's father was a railroad conductor. Hutson had two younger brothers. In 1935, he married Julia Richards. They had three daughters.

....

EDUCATION Hutson graduated from the University of Alabama.

....

AWARDS Awarded the Joe F. Carr Trophy as NFL MVP in 1941 and 1942, 1930s All-Decade team, NFL All-Time team, inducted into the Pro Football Hall of Fame in 1963

Don Hutson
End

Early Years

Don Hutson only played one year of high school football. In his senior year, his friend Bob Seawell convinced him to try out for the team. Hutson had a good season, but university teams were more interested in his friend. Seawell agreed to play for the University of Alabama, but only if Hutson came with him.

Hutson was known for his speed. By his senior year in university, he was nicknamed the "Alabama Antelope." Hutson was named to the All-American team in his senior year. After graduating from university in 1935, he signed a **contract** to play with the Green Bay Packers.

Developing Skills

Hutson was the first player to create a series of moves and fakes to get away from opposing defenders. He is credited with inventing modern pass receiving. Many of the pass routes Hutson created, including the **z-out** and **buttonhook**, are still used today. In 1942, Hutson caught 74 passes for 1,211 yards and 17 touchdowns.

Hutson finished his football career with 99 touchdown catches. This record stood for more than four decades. After 11 seasons of play, he had a total of 18 NFL records. At that time, his record of 488 career receptions was more than 200 ahead of his next closest competitor. He led the NFL in receiving for eight of 11 years. Hutson holds eight NFL records that stand today. These records include leading the league in scoring for five straight seasons and nine seasons of leading the league in receiving touchdowns.

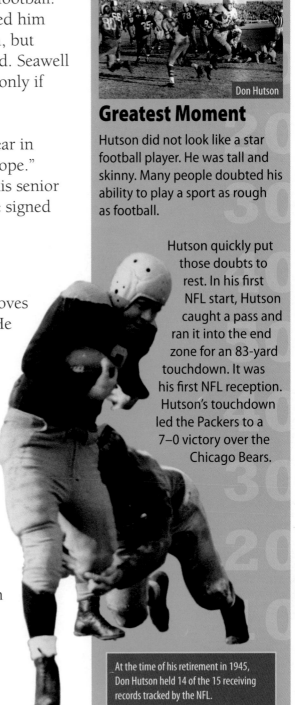

Don Hutson

Greatest Moment

Hutson did not look like a star football player. He was tall and skinny. Many people doubted his ability to play a sport as rough as football.

Hutson quickly put those doubts to rest. In his first NFL start, Hutson caught a pass and ran it into the end zone for an 83-yard touchdown. It was his first NFL reception. Hutson's touchdown led the Packers to a 7–0 victory over the Chicago Bears.

At the time of his retirement in 1945, Don Hutson held 14 of the 15 receiving records tracked by the NFL.

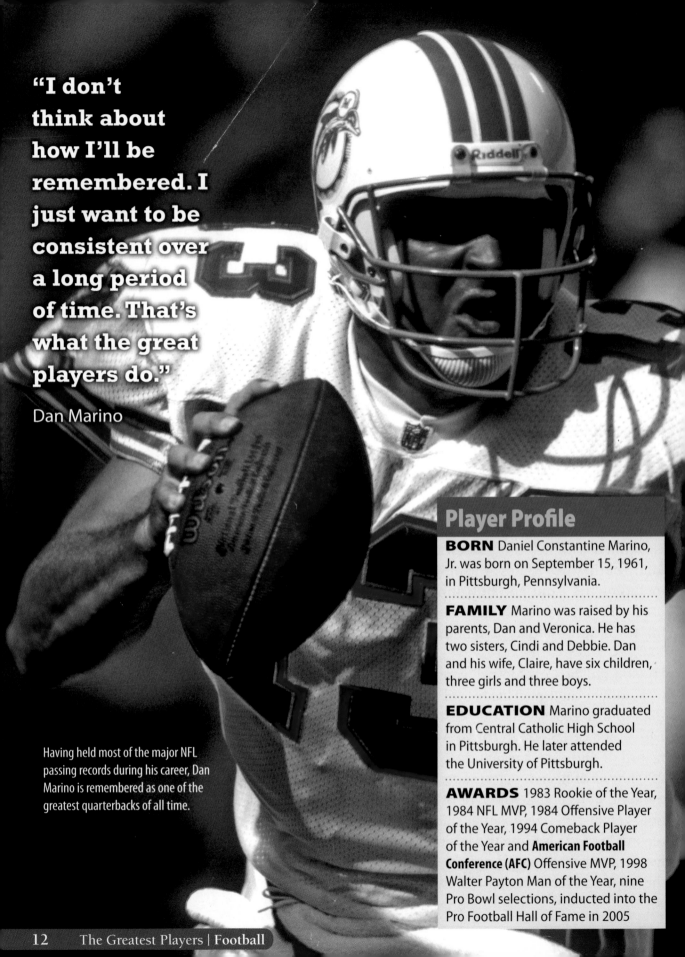

"I don't think about how I'll be remembered. I just want to be consistent over a long period of time. That's what the great players do."

Dan Marino

Having held most of the major NFL passing records during his career, Dan Marino is remembered as one of the greatest quarterbacks of all time.

Player Profile

BORN Daniel Constantine Marino, Jr. was born on September 15, 1961, in Pittsburgh, Pennsylvania.

FAMILY Marino was raised by his parents, Dan and Veronica. He has two sisters, Cindi and Debbie. Dan and his wife, Claire, have six children, three girls and three boys.

EDUCATION Marino graduated from Central Catholic High School in Pittsburgh. He later attended the University of Pittsburgh.

AWARDS 1983 Rookie of the Year, 1984 NFL MVP, 1984 Offensive Player of the Year, 1994 Comeback Player of the Year and **American Football Conference (AFC)** Offensive MVP, 1998 Walter Payton Man of the Year, nine Pro Bowl selections, inducted into the Pro Football Hall of Fame in 2005

Dan Marino
Quarterback

Early Years

Dan Marino was a star athlete in his teens. He was quarterback for the Vikings of Pittsburgh's Central Catholic High School. In his senior year of high school, he was drafted to play Major League Baseball for the Kansas City Royals. Instead, he decided to play university football.

Playing for the University of Pittsburgh, Marino set National Collegiate Athletic Association (NCAA) season and career records for pass attempts and completions, passing yards gained, and touchdowns. In 1982, the university retired Marino's jersey number.

Developing Skills

In 1983, Marino earned a starting role with the Miami Dolphins early in his rookie season. The next season, he set NFL records with 5,084 passing yards and 48 touchdowns. He was the first player ever to pass for 5,000 yards in a single season, and his 48 touchdown passes shattered the previous record of 36.

In 1986, Marino threw for 4,746 yards and 44 touchdowns. He became the only quarterback to throw 40 or more touchdowns in a season twice. By 1995, Marino became the career passing leader in attempts, completions, yards, and touchdowns. Thirteen times in his career, Marino passed for 3,000 yards or more in one season. He threw for 400 or more yards in a single game another 13 times. Marino retired at the end of the 1999 season.

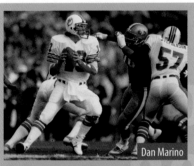
Dan Marino

Greatest Moment

For many football players, their greatest moment comes in the final game that takes the team to the Super Bowl. Sometimes, it comes in the Super Bowl itself. Marino only played in one Super Bowl game, losing to the San Francisco 49ers in 1984.

Instead, Marino's greatest moment may have been when he stood back and looked at his career. It included 4,967 completed passes for 61,361 yards and 420 touchdowns. He retired with 54 Dolphin team records and 22 NFL records. He still holds nine NFL records, including most seasons leading the league in pass completions (6) and yards gained (5).

Dan Marino ranks second on the NFL all-time leaders list in six categories. Only Brett Favre has recorded more career completed passes, passing yards gained, and touchdown passes.

"Winners, I am convinced, imagine their dreams first. They want it with all their heart and expect it to come true. There is, I believe, no other way to live."

Joe Montana

Joe Montana is the NFL's only three-time Super Bowl MVP.

Player Profile

BORN Joseph Clifford Montana, Jr. was born on June 11, 1956, in New Eagle, Pennsylvania.

FAMILY Montana was raised by parents Theresa and Joe Montana, Sr. He is married and has four children with his wife, Jennifer.

EDUCATION Montana graduated from Ringgold High School. He later attended the University of Notre Dame.

AWARDS Three Super Bowl MVP awards, two NFL MVP awards, 1986 Co-Comeback Player of the Year, 1989 Offensive Player of the Year, eight Pro Bowl selections, 1980s All-Decade team, NFL All-Time Team, inducted into the Pro Football Hall of Fame in 2000

Joe Montana
Quarterback

Early Years

From the time he was a child, Joe Montana loved sports. He waited at night for his dad to come home from work so they could play catch with a football or baseball. He practiced his aim by throwing balls through tire swings. Montana was also a good basketball player. In fact, he was so good at basketball that he was offered a scholarship to North Carolina State University.

However, football became Montana's passion when he became a starting quarterback in high school. In his senior year, he accepted a scholarship to play football at the University of Notre Dame.

Developing Skills

During his first two seasons at Notre Dame, Montana did not see much action. That changed after he led the team to two comeback wins. He was nicknamed "The Comeback Kid." Montana earned the role of starting quarterback and led his team to wins in the 1978 and 1979 **Cotton Bowl**.

In 1979, Montana was drafted by the San Francisco 49ers. Halfway through the 1980 season, he became the starting quarterback after leading the team to a fourth-quarter comeback victory over the New Orleans Saints. "The Comeback Kid" led his team to a fourth-quarter comeback win another 30 times in his professional career. Montana led San Francisco to four Super Bowl championships. In 1995, he retired with 3,409 completions, 40,551 yards, 273 touchdowns, and a 92.3 **passer rating**.

Joe Montana

Greatest Moment

One of Montana's greatest moments came during the 1982 **National Football Conference (NFC)** Championship game against the Dallas Cowboys. Trailing 27–21 with less than five minutes left on the clock, Montana led his team on a long fourth-quarter drive. He threw seven successful passes and handed off another four runs to bring the 49ers to the Cowboys' 6-yard line. The drive ended with Montana completing a touchdown pass to Dwight Clark to tie the game. After kicking for the **extra point**, the 49ers won 28–27.

Joe Montana holds the all-time NFL record for most Super Bowl touchdown passes (45), most playoff completed passes (460), and most playoff yards gained (5,772).

> "I want to be remembered as the guy who gave his all whenever he was on the field."

Walter Payton

Walter Payton was the most dominant running back of the 1970s and 1980s. During that time, he set 14 NFL records, including most career rushing touchdowns (110) and most rushing yards gained in a single game (275).

Player Profile

BORN Walter Jerry Payton was born on July 25, 1954, in Columbia, Mississippi.

FAMILY Payton spent his childhood with his brother, sister, and parents, Peter and Alyne Payton. He married Connie Norwood in 1976. The couple had a daughter, Brittney, and a son, Jarrett.

EDUCATION Payton graduated from Columbia High School. He later graduated from Jackson State University with a degree in communications and special education.

AWARDS 1977 NFL MVP, 1978 Pro Bowl MVP, NFC Offensive Player of the Year in 1977 and 1985, nine Pro Bowl selections, NFL All-Time team, inducted into the Pro Football Hall of Fame in 1993

Walter Payton
Running Back

Early Years

Walter Payton was a natural athlete. In his first year of high school, Payton was a track and field star. He won the state long jump title that year. By his third year of high school, a coach convinced him to give football a try. Payton later earned a spot on the All-State football team.

In 1972, Payton started attending Jackson State University. It was here that his football career really began. During his college years, Payton set a school rushing record of 3,563 yards. He scored 66 touchdowns and once scored 46 points in one game. His play was noticed by the Chicago Bears, who drafted him in 1975.

Developing Skills

"Sweetness" is an unusual nickname for a football player. It was given to the 5-foot 10-inch tall, 200-pound player because of his smooth moves on the field. He was anything but "sweet" as he ran through or around tacklers. Payton is credited with inventing the stutter-step, a high-stepping run with an irregular pace. He used this running technique to confuse defenders.

In his 13-year career, Payton became an all-time NFL leader in rushing and combined yards. In 1985, he rushed for 1,551 yards and helped lead the Chicago Bears to their first and only Super Bowl victory. When Payton left the game in 1987, the Bears retired his number 34. Payton finished his career with 16,726 rushing yards and 110 rushing touchdowns. He added another 4,538 receiving yards off 492 receptions and 15 touchdown catches.

Walter Payton

Greatest Moment

It was October 7, 1984. The Chicago Bears were hosting the New Orleans Saints. There was more on the line than just winning or losing on this day. Payton was about to break the NFL record for rushing yards. The record of 12,312 rushing yards was set 19 years earlier by Jim Brown.

In the second half, Payton grabbed the ball and squeezed through the offensive line for a "sweet" six-yard gain. That was the record-breaking rush. He finished the game with 154 rushing yards.

In 1985, Walter Payton led the Chicago Bears to their best ever season. They posted a record of 15 wins and one loss that year. The team ended the season with its first Super Bowl championship.

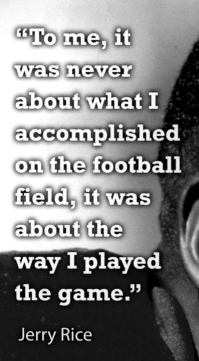

> "To me, it was never about what I accomplished on the football field, it was about the way I played the game."

Jerry Rice

Jerry Rice holds nearly every major record for a wide receiver in the NFL. In 2010, the NFL ranked Rice as the number 1 greatest player in league history.

Player Profile

BORN Jerry Lee Rice was born on October 13, 1962, in Crawford, Mississippi.

FAMILY Rice was one of eight children born to Joe Nathan and Eddie Rice. Rice and his wife, Jackie, have two girls, Jacqui and Jada, and one boy, Jerry, Jr.

EDUCATION Rice graduated from B.L. Moor High School in Crawford. He later attended Mississippi Valley State University.

AWARDS 1987 NFL MVP, 1987 Bert Bell Award for Player of the Year, 1989 Super Bowl MVP, 1990 Player of the Year, two-time NFL Offensive Player of the Year, Three-time NFC Offensive Player of the Year, 1996 Pro Bowl MVP, 13 Pro Bowl selections, 1980s All-Decade Team, 1990s All-Decade Team, NFL All-Time Team, inducted into the Pro Football Hall of Fame in 2010

Jerry Rice
Wide Receiver

Early Years

Jerry Rice did not start playing football until his second year of high school. He played many different positions, including defensive back, wide receiver, and kick returner. He eventually became an All-State player, and received offers to play for several university teams.

In 1984, Rice was a senior at Mississippi Valley State University. That season, he broke college football records with 1,845 receiving yards, 112 receptions, and 27 touchdowns. In total, Rice broke or set 18 records during his university career.

Developing Skills

In 1985, Rice was drafted by the San Francisco 49ers. His rookie year had a shaky start. He dropped a record 15 passes that year, but he also set a team record for 241 receiving yards in one game. In 1986, he had 15 touchdowns and averaged 18.3 yards per catch. The next year was even better. Rice set NFL records with 22 receiving touchdowns and 13 straight games with a touchdown catch. He set a team record of 138 points that season.

Following two Super Bowl wins in 1989 and 1990, there was no holding Rice back. In 1992, he broke the career touchdown reception record when he caught his 101st touchdown pass. Rice later played with the Oakland Raiders and the Seattle Seahawks before retiring in 2005. He left the game with career records of 1,549 catches for 22,895 yards, a career average of 14.8 yards per catch, and 208 touchdowns.

Jerry Rice

Greatest Moment

Rice suffered a sprained ankle shortly before the 1989 Super Bowl. The injury was so bad that he was not expected to play in the game.

Rice decided to play. The 49ers were losing 13–6 to the Cincinnati Bengals in the fourth quarter when Rice caught a pass from quarterback Joe Montana in the end zone to tie the game at 13–13. Then, with just over a minute left in the game, Rice caught a 27-yard pass to set up the game-winning touchdown. The 49ers won 20–16, and Rice was voted Super Bowl MVP.

Jerry Rice holds 38 all-time NFL records, including Super Bowl records for most receiving yards in a game (215) and most receiving touchdowns in a game (3). He is also ranked second or third in another 17 record categories.

> **"There were probably about five games in my career where everything was moving in slow motion and you could be out there all day, totally in the zone."**
>
> Lawrence Taylor

Lawrence Taylor is widely considered the greatest defensive player in NFL history. Many opposing coaches developed strategies just for dealing with Taylor.

Player Profile

BORN Lawrence Julius Taylor was born on February 4, 1959, in Williamsburg, Virginia.

FAMILY Taylor was the middle of three boys born to Clarence and Iris Taylor. He was married and had four children.

EDUCATION Taylor graduated from Lafayette High School. He later attended the University of North Carolina.

AWARDS 1986 NFL MVP, 1986 Bert Bell Award as Player of the Year, 1981 Rookie of the Year, 1981 Defensive Rookie of the Year, three-time Defensive Player of the Year, 1986 NFC Defensive Player of the Year, 10 Pro Bowl selections, 1980s All-Decade Team, NFL All-Time Team, inducted into the Pro Football Hall of Fame in 1999

Lawrence Taylor
Linebacker

Early Years

Lawrence Taylor never excelled at school, but he did well in sports. Fearing the dangers of playing a sport as rough as football, Taylor's parents originally signed him up to play baseball. He played four seasons of baseball before a high school football coach talked him into switching sports.

Taylor graduated from high school in 1977. He accepted a scholarship from the University of North Carolina and joined the school football team. Taylor started as a defensive lineman but later moved to linebacker in 1979. The next year, he recorded 16 **sacks** and was named the Atlantic Coast Conference Player of the Year and an All-American. In 1981, he was drafted by the New York Giants.

Developing Skills

Taylor finished his rookie year with 133 tackles and 9.5 sacks. He was named Rookie of the Year and elected to the All-Pro team. Despite many serious personal problems, he continued to play well. In 1986, the Giants won the Super Bowl. Taylor set a Giants' record that season with 20.5 sacks. He added 105 tackles, two forced fumbles, and five blocked passes. In his first 10 years in the NFL, Taylor was named to the Pro Bowl every year.

The end of the decade saw a slump in the star player's game. In 1991, however, Taylor and the Giants won the Super Bowl. They defeated the favored Buffalo Bills 20-19 to claim the championship. Taylor retired after the 1993 season with a record of 132.5 career sacks. He also recorded 1,088 tackles and 33 forced fumbles during his career.

Lawrence Taylor

Greatest Moment

It was 1988, and the New York Giants were in New Orleans to take on the Saints. Taylor was suffering from torn muscles in his chest and shoulder. He struggled to get into a sling and harness to keep his shoulder in place. Then, Taylor played the game of his life. He recorded seven tackles, three sacks, and two forced fumbles. Taylor's great play helped lead the Giants to a tight 13-12 victory.

If sacks had been an officially counted statistic in 1981, Lawrence Taylor's career sack total would be 142. This would place him in the top five all-time sack leaders.

"There is a difference between conceit and confidence. Conceit is bragging about yourself. Confidence means you believe you can get the job done."

Johnny Unitas

For the NFL's 50th anniversary in 1969, Johnny Unitas was voted the greatest quarterback of all time. When he retired in 1973, he held 22 NFL all-time records.

Player Profile

BORN John Constantine Unitas was born on May 7, 1933, in Pittsburgh, Pennsylvania.

FAMILY Unitas was the third of four children born to parents Leon and Helen Unitas.

EDUCATION Unitas graduated from St. Justin's High School. He later attended the University of Louisville.

AWARDS Three NFL MVP awards, 1970 NFL Man of the Year, three Bert Bell Awards as Player of the Year Award, 10 Pro Bowl selections, three Pro Bowl MVP awards, 1960s All-Decade Team, NFL All-Time Team, inducted into the Pro Football Hall of Fame in 1979

Johnny Unitas
Quarterback

Early Years

When Johnny Unitas was four years old, his father died of pneumonia. He grew up watching his mother work hard to support the family. At age 12, Unitas was determined to become a professional football player. In his senior year, he became quarterback on Pittsburgh's All-Catholic High School team. In 1951, Unitas attended the University of Louisville. At 6 feet tall and 138 pounds, the coaches thought he was too small for college football. By the time he graduated in 1955, however, Unitas had grown an inch taller and gained almost 60 pounds.

In 1955, Unitas was drafted by the Pittsburgh Steelers, but he was cut from the team during training camp. He then played on a semi-professional team in New Jersey. Reports of his talent spread quickly, and he was offered a position as backup quarterback for the Baltimore Colts.

Developing Skills

In the fourth game of the 1956 season, Unitas finally got a chance to play. By the end of the season, he earned the starting quarterback position. In 1957, Unitas led the NFL in passing yards and touchdown passes. The following year, he led the Colts to the NFL championship. The team would win again the following year.

Unitas' reputation as a leader and passer was well-deserved. He threw at least one touchdown pass in 47 consecutive games. This record still stands. Unitas also held the record for most Pro Bowl appearances by a quarterback until 2009, when Brett Favre passed him.

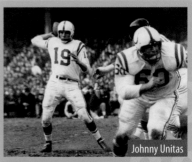
Johnny Unitas

Greatest Moment

On December 28, 1958, Unitas led the Baltimore Colts to the NFL championship over the New York Giants. The game was decided in a sudden death overtime at Yankee Stadium. It was the first NFL game ever to be decided this way. The game is now commonly known as "The Greatest Game Ever Played."

With two minutes left to play in the fourth quarter, Unitas led a charge that set up a field goal to tie the game. In overtime, Unitas led the Colts 80 yards down the field to score the winning touchdown. The final score was 23–17.

About 45 million people watched the 1958 NFL championship on TV. The game is credited with raising the popularity of football in the United States.

"A lot of people look at athletes as role models, and to be successful as an athlete, I've got to do what I do, hard but fair... I try to live a certain way, and maybe that'll have some kind of effect."

Reggie White

At the time of his retirement in 2000, Reggie White held most of the major NFL sack records, including most career sacks (198) and most consecutive seasons with 10 or more sacks (9).

Player Profile

BORN Reginald Howard White was born on December 19, 1961, in Chattanooga, Tennessee.

FAMILY White was born to Thelma Kire and Charles White. White and his wife, Sara, had two children, Jeremy and Jecolia.

EDUCATION White graduated from Howard High School. He later graduated from the University of Tennessee with a degree in human services.

AWARDS 1985 Defensive Rookie of the Year, 1986 First-Team All-NFL award, two-time Defensive Player of the Year, three NFC Defensive Player of the Year awards, 13 Pro Bowl selections, 1986 Pro Bowl MVP, 1980s All-Decade Team, 1990s All-Decade team, NFL All-Time Team, inducted into the Pro Football Hall of Fame in 2006

Reggie White
Defensive End

Early Years

When Reggie White was 12 years old, he told his mother that he was going to be both a preacher and a professional football player when he grew up. Five years later, he was ordained as a Baptist minister. White played college football after graduating from high school. By his senior year in 1983, he was named Southeastern Conference Player of the Year.

In 1984, White was drafted by the Memphis Showboats of the United States Football League (USFL). He was 22 years old. At 6 feet 5 inches tall and 291 pounds, no one wanted to mess with the "Minister of Defense." White was voted to the USFL All-Rookie team in his first season. He left the USFL and joined the NFL's Philadelphia Eagles in 1985.

Developing Skills

In 1986, White recorded 18 sacks during the regular season and another four sacks at the Pro Bowl. In 1987, he led the league with 21 sacks. In the first game of the season, White showed the range of his talent when he took the ball from the quarterback and ran 70 yards for a touchdown.

In 1993, White joined the Green Bay Packers. He led the Packers' defense from 23rd place to 2nd place in his first year. During the 1997 Super Bowl, he set a record of three sacks.

White retired after the 1998 season. In 2000, he played one last season with the Carolina Panthers. White died in 2004. He was only 43 years old.

Reggie White

Greatest Moment

One of White's greatest moments was actually an entire football season. His performance in the 1987 NFL season stands as one of the most dominant defensive seasons ever played.

Due to a player strike, the 1987 NFL season was shortened to just 12 games. Despite losing four games to the strike, White set an NFL record of 21 sacks in just 12 games. Only two players have ever recorded more sacks in one season, and they both needed a full 16 games to do it. White finished the season with 76 tackles, four forced fumbles, a fumble recovery, and one touchdown.

In eight seasons with the Philadelphia Eagles, Reggie White recorded more sacks than games played. During that time, he had 124 sacks in 121 games.

Greatest Moments

1958 – The Greatest Game Ever Played

When: December 28, 1958

Where: New York, New York

The 1958 NFL championship between the New York Giants and the Baltimore Colts was the first NFL game to be decided by sudden death overtime. With the ball on their own 14 yard line, Johnny Unitas led the Colts to within 13 yards of the end zone. Steve Myhra kicked a field goal to tie the game with just seven seconds left. In overtime, Unitas led the Colts 80 yards down the field in 13 plays. The Colts won 23-17.

1958
Johnny Unitas leads the Baltimore Colts to victory in "The Greatest Game Ever Played."

1965
Jim Brown becomes the first NFL player to score 100 rushing touchdowns.

1920	1930	1940	1950	1960

1972 – The Immaculate Reception

When: December 23, 1972

Where: Pittsburgh, Pennsylvania

The Pittsburgh Steelers trailed the Oakland Raiders 7-6 with 22 seconds left on the clock. Steelers quarterback Terry Bradshaw had time for one last pass. The pass was intended for halfback Frenchy Fuqua, but when Fuqua tried to make the catch he collided with Raiders defender Jack Tatum. The ball bounced off Fuqua and Tatum, and it was about to hit the ground when Steelers running back Franco Harris caught the ball and ran it into the end zone to score the game-winning touchdown. The catch is considered one of the greatest plays in NFL history.

1935
Don Hutson completes an 83-yard touchdown reception on the first catch of his NFL career.

1973
Dick Butkus plays in his eighth straight Pro Bowl before his career comes to an early end due to injury.

1987
Walter Payton retires from football as the league leader in career rushing yards.

1982 – The Catch

When: January 10, 1982

Where: San Francisco, California

In the NFC championship, the Dallas Cowboys led the San Francisco 49ers by six points in the final minute of the game. The 49ers were six yards from the end zone. Then, 49ers quarterback Joe Montana released a high pass to the back of the end zone. San Francisco receiver Dwight Clark jumped and stretched out to reach the ball. Clark managed to pull the ball in, scoring the game-winning touchdown for the home team. The play is now known simply as "the catch."

1984
Dan Marino becomes the first quarterback to throw for more than 5,000 yards in a season.

1989
Joe Montana sets an NFL record when he is named Super Bowl MVP for the third time.

1997
Reggie White sets a Super Bowl record for most sacks in a game.

1970   1980   1990   2000   2010

1988
Jerry Rice sets a Super Bowl record with 215 receiving yards on his way to being named Super Bowl MVP.

1988
Lawrence Taylor plays with a torn muscle but still manages to record seven quarterback sacks.

2000 – The Tackle

When: January 31, 2000

Where: Atlanta, Georgia

The 1999 Super Bowl was a hard-fought battle between the St. Louis Rams and Tennessee Titans. The Rams built a 16-0 lead before the Titans kicked off the biggest comeback in Super Bowl history. The Titans tied the game at 16. Then, with about 2 minutes left, Rams quarterback Kurt Warner completed a 73-yard touchdown pass to take the lead. With six seconds left, Titans receiver Kenny Dyson caught a pass and headed for the end zone. Dyson was less than one yard away from tying the game when Rams linebacker Mike Jones tackled him. The tackle secured the first Super Bowl victory for the Rams.

27

Write a Biography

Life Story

A person's life story can be the subject of a book. This kind of book is called a biography. Biographies often describe the lives of people who have achieved great success. These people may be alive today, or they may have lived many years ago. Reading a biography can help you learn more about a great person.

Get the Facts

Use this book, and research in the library and on the Internet, to find out more about your favorite football player. Learn as much about this player as you can. What team did this person play for? What are his or her statistics in important categories? Has this person set any records? Be sure to also write down key events in the person's life. What was this person's childhood like? What has he or she accomplished? Is there anything else that makes this person special or unusual?

Use the Concept Web

A concept web is a useful research tool. Read the questions in the concept web on the following page. Answer the questions in your notebook. Your answers will help you write a biography.

Brett Favre holds most of the all-time NFL records for quarterbacks, include most completed passes (6,083), most passing yards (69,329), and most touchdown passes (497).

Concept Web

- What did you learn from the books you read in your research?
- Would you suggest these books to others?
- Was anything missing from these books?

- Where does this individual currently reside?
- Does he or she have a family?

- Where and when was this person born?
- Describe his or her parents, siblings, and friends.
- Did this person grow up in unusual circumstances?

Your Opinion

Adulthood

Childhood

WRITING A BIOGRAPHY

Main Accomplishments

Help and Obstacles

Work and Preparation

- What is this person's life's work?
- Has he or she received awards or recognition for accomplishments?
- How have this person's accomplishments served others?

- What was this person's education?
- What was his or her work experience?
- How does this person work; what is the process he or she uses?

- Did this individual have a positive attitude?
- Did he or she receive help from others?
- Did this person have a mentor?
- Did this person face any hardships?
- If so, how were the hardships overcome?

Know your STUFF!

1 Who was the first running back to score 100 rushing touchdowns?

2 How many tackles did Dick Butkus record in his first NFL game?

3 Who is credited with inventing modern pass receiving techniques?

4 What records did Dan Marino set in his first full year as a starting quarterback?

5 Who is the only quarterback to be named Super Bowl MVP three times?

6 Which running back was given the nickname "the sweetness"?

7 Which San Francisco 49er played the 1989 Super Bowl on a sprained ankle to help his team win the championship?

8 What honors did Lawrence Taylor win in his first season in the NFL?

9 What is "The greatest game ever played"?

10 What record does Reggie White still hold?

ANSWERS: 1. Jim Brown 2. 11 3. Don Hutson 4. First quarterback to throw for 5,000 yards and 48 touchdowns 5. Joe Montana 6. Walter Payton 7. Jerry Rice 8. Rookie of the Year, Defensive Player of the Year, and named to the All-Pro team 9. The 1958 NFL championship game between the New York Giants and the Baltimore Colts 10. Most quarterback sacks in 12 games

Glossary

American Football Conference (AFC): one of two conferences that make up the NFL

Big Ten Championship: annual college football game to determine the season champion of the Big Ten Conference, which is made up of teams from Midwestern United States colleges and universities

buttonhook: a route run by a receiver; involved running a set number of steps or yards before quickly turning back to look for a pass

contract: a written agreement to play for a certain team

Cotton Bowl: an annual football game played between two of the top college teams

end zone: the area at each end of the field in which offensive players try to enter to score points

extra point: additional points earned by a team after scoring a touchdown; either a kick for one point or a run or catch to the end zone for two points

field goal: an attempt to kick the ball through the goalposts to score three points

first down: the first of four chances to gain 10 yards; once 10 yards is gained, the offense is granted another first down

fumbles: when the ball carrier drops the ball

interception: a pass caught by a defending player

Most Valuable Player (MVP): the player judged to be the most valuable to his team's success

National Football Conference (NFC): one of two conferences that make up the NFL

passer rating: a number given to quarterbacks to help judge their ability in the position; based on many statistics, including passes completed and interceptions thrown

Pro Bowl: a game played each year between the NFL's best players, or all-stars

sacks: when defensive players bring down a quarterback for a loss of yards

tackle: to forcefully bring an opposing player to a stop through bodily contact

touchdown: when a team enters the opposing team's end zone with the ball; worth six points

z-out: a route run by a receiver who follows a z-shaped pattern down the field

Index

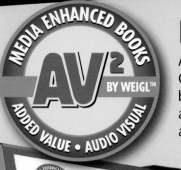

Log on to www.av2books.com

AV² by Weigl brings you media enhanced books that support active learning. Go to www.av2books.com, and enter the special code found on page 2 of this book. You will gain access to enriched and enhanced content that supplements and complements this book. Content includes video, audio, web links, quizzes, a slide show, and activities.

Audio
Listen to sections of the book read aloud.

Video
Watch informative video clips.

Embedded Weblinks
Gain additional information for research.

Try This!
Complete activities and hands-on experiments.

WHAT'S ONLINE?

Try This!	**Embedded Weblinks**	**Video**	**EXTRA FEATURES**
Try a football activity.	Learn more about football players.	Watch a video about football.	**Audio** Listen to sections of the book read aloud.
Test your knowledge of football equipment.	Read about football coaches.	View football stars in action.	**Key Words** Study vocabulary, and complete a matching word activity.
Complete a mapping activity.	Find more information about where football games take place.	Watch a video about football players.	**Slide Show** View images and captions, and prepare a presentation.
			Quizzes Test your knowledge.

AV² was built to bridge the gap between print and digital. We encourage you to tell us what you like and what you want to see in the future.
Sign up to be an AV² Ambassador at www.av2books.com/ambassador.